Chicken Soup for the Soul®
Cartoons for Golfers

CHICKEN SOUP
FOR THE SOUL®
CARTOONS FOR GOLFERS

Jack Canfield
Mark Victor Hansen
John McPherson
Creator of *Close to Home*

Health Communications, Inc.
Deerfield Beach, Florida

www.hcibooks.com
www.chickensoup.com

CLOSE TO HOME ©2003 *John McPherson. Reprinted with permission of Universal Press Syndicate.* www.ucomics.com.

For information on reprinting any cartoons in this book, please go to *www.amureprints.com.*

**Library of Congress Cataloging-in-Publication Data
is available from the Library of Congress.**

©2005 Jack Canfield and Mark Victor Hansen
ISBN 0-7573-0267-X

Publisher: Health Communications, Inc.
          3201 S.W. 15th Street
          Deerfield Beach, Florida 33442-8190

Cover design by Larissa Hise Henoch
Inside formatting by Dawn Von Strolley Grove

Other books by John McPherson

Chicken Soup for the Soul® Cartoons for Moms
Chicken Soup for the Soul® Cartoons for Teachers
Chicken Soup for the Soul® Cartoons for Dads
Close to Home
Dangerously Close to Home
One Step Closer to Home
The Silence of the Lamberts
Close to Home Revisited
Home: The Final Frontier
Close to Home Unplugged
Striking Close to Home
The Close to Home Survival Guide
The Get Well Book
High School Isn't Pretty
Close to Home Uncut
The Scourge of Vinyl Car Seats
Close to Home Exposed
The Honeymoon Is Over

Acknowledgments

We wish to express our heartfelt gratitude to the following people who helped make this book possible:

Our publisher Peter Vegso, for his vision and commitment to bringing *Chicken Soup for the Soul* to the world.

Patty Aubery and Russ Kamalski, for being there on every step of the journey, with love, laughter and endless creativity.

Patty Hansen and Dena Jacobson, for their thorough and competent handling of the legal and licensing aspects of the *Chicken Soup for the Soul* books. You are both magnificent at the challenge!

Laurie Hartman, for being a precious guardian of the *Chicken Soup* brand.

Jack and Mark's wonderful staff who support their businesses with skill and love. Thanks to Veronica Romero, D'ette Corona, Jesse Ianniello, Barbara LoMonaco, Teresa Esparza, Robin Yerian, Jody Emme, Trudy Marschall, Michelle Adams, Dee Dee Romanello, Shanna Vieyra, Lisa Williams, Gina Romanello, Brittany Shaw, Tanya Jones, Mary McKay and David Coleman.

Allison Janse, Elizabeth Rinaldi, Kathy Grant and Bret Witter, our editors at Health Communications, Inc., for their devotion to excellence.

Terry Burke and the marketing and PR departments at Health Communications, Inc., for doing such an incredible job supporting our books.

The art department at Health Communications, Inc., for their talent, creativity and unrelenting patience in producing book covers and inside designs that capture the essence of *Chicken Soup*: Larissa Hise Henoch, Lawna Patterson Oldfield, Andrea Perrine Brower, Anthony Clausi and Dawn Grove.

Thank you to all of the *Chicken Soup for the Soul* coauthors, who make it so much of a joy to be part of this *Chicken Soup* family.

To Greg Melvin, Lee Salem, Denise Clark and the other great folks at Universal Press Syndicate for their ongoing support of John and his work.

Special thanks to John Vivona and the Universal Press sales force for their hard work on John's behalf. You guys are the best.

Lastly, thanks to Chris Millis, John's right-hand man.

We are truly grateful and love you all!

Introduction

Golf is many things to many people; but, most of all, it is a mirror. And when we look into that mirror we cannot help but see our lives and ourselves, not the way we would like them to be, but the way they really *are*. Fortunately the wisdom gained from the game helps us find the lighter side of that all-too-honest view. Whether knee-slapping hilarious or just chuckle-to-yourself funny, no other sport can boast of its ability to make us laugh the way golf can—because golf forces us to laugh at ourselves.

If you're reading this, chances are you're a golfer, which means that any of the following will strike a chord or make you grin, and possibly even make you laugh till it hurts:

- You find yourself wishing you could meet the rest of your four-some with your handy-dandy automated applause system in tow.
- You convince yourself that a windmill—blocked by dense foliage, perhaps, but somewhere nearby nonetheless—must be responsible for that one hole you can't ever make.
- You fantasize about an anti-slice device that looks like a super-sized version of a kids' crazy straw.

- You yell "Fore!" when you see an asteroid-sized ball speeding directly toward your head. (After all, it's the most amazing thing you ever witnessed—what else would you do . . . run for cover?)

We relate to all this because golf makes us face our own shortcomings in a way that other sports, even other solitary ones, just can't. Take swimming, diving or skiing: nothing funny about swallowing water or crashing into a snowbound tree. But spontaneously leaping for joy because you had three witnesses to your hole-in-one—now *that's* something to make you beam from ear to ear, laugh joyfully in perfect understanding, and even sing! (Yes, sing! You *are* a golfer, aren't you?)

We hope you'll agree that the cartoons in this collection capture all the magic, delight and humor of the game, and celebrate just why you love it so much. Whether it's walking on the green, swinging a perfectly balanced titanium driver, or reaching the Zen state only putting can create, nothing puts a smile on a golfer's face like, well, playing golf! May this book bring you as much joy as the game of golf itself.

To this dismay of his fellow golfers, Jerry
outfitted himself with an automated applause system.

"The pro told me they just laid off nine greenskeepers. He wants us to swerve around as much as possible while we play."

*The reason the pro tells you to keep your head down
is so you can't see him laughing.*

Phyllis Diller

With the help of acupuncture, Gary was able
to trim 11 strokes off his game.

"It was custom-made to counteract my slice!"

"Only one of them is the real hole. The others
are decoys, with Plexiglas covering the holes."

"Whoa! Don't help him, Mike. According to this note, he burped, causing another golfer in his foursome to miss a 2-foot eagle putt."

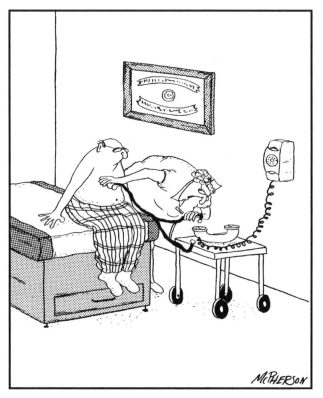

"Go ahead and tee off. Then I want
you to listen to this wheezing."

"Yep, it's yours, all right! Top-Flite
three! Tough break, hombre!"

Dave hadn't lost a ball in seven years.

"*That* was the sound of a custom-made graphite 5-iron going through a 10-horsepower chipper! Let's listen to a titanium driver! Or are you *finally* in the mood to wallpaper the kitchen?!"

When it's breezy hit it easy.

Davis Love Jr.

"One, it's at least three miles away! Two, there's only a 40 percent chance that it'll come this way. Three, I'm 2 under par through 12 holes!"

"This'll just take a second. It was
my husband's last request."

Tiger Woods: the early months.

"Head down the right side about 150 yards. If my
drive slices, just deflect it back onto
the fairway toward the green."

The face of golf is changed forever with the
invention of mobile, dimple-sensing sand traps.

"In keeping with Dan's last request, each of you may
toss a handful of golf balls onto the casket while
Dan receives a 21-titanium-driver salute."

Russ foolishly ordered the Sense-a-tron option
when he signed up for the Weather Channel.

"OK, fine! If that's the way you wanna play,
I'll make obnoxious gurgling sounds the
next time *you're* putting for birdie!"

The emerging and exhilarating sport of Ice Golf.

"I'm serious. Swing as hard as you can.
It's impossible to slice."

My worst day of golf still beats my best day at the office.

John Hallisey

"I see the ball starting out five inches left of center, struck lightly, it gathers speed down a long incline, bends right . . . and into the center of the cup."

With a built-in 300-watt amplifier, Phil's new
KA-BOOM™ driver did an amazing job at
intimidating opponents.

"He hasn't lost a ball in two years."

"Lois, I am fine! We planned this golf vacation
two years ago! If you think I'm going to let
a little back trouble ruin it, you're crazy!"

"Now THAT is what I call a tough approach shot!"

"I hate this hole."

"Boy, that's a shame. Pouring rain when you wanted to play more golf. Well, seems like a good opportunity to paint the living room."

"Through the clown's belly, play it as it lies.
Through his nose, deduct one stroke.
Through his mouth, deduct three strokes."

Your financial cost can best be figured out when you realize that if you were to devote the same time and energy to business instead of golf, you'd be a millionaire in approximately six weeks.

Buddy Hackett

Chuck was having a difficult time
transitioning into retirement.

"OK, you can golf. But here's the deal. You break 90
and you can play poker on Wednesday. Anything over 90
and you have to scrape and paint the house."

Having tried for years to put some zest
into their marriage, Carol finally turns Leon's head
with her new Top-Flite teddy.

When I die, bury me on the golf course so my husband will visit.

Author Unknown

The IRS embarks on a tough new
approach to audits.

"You're being sued by Mr. Gertman for $1.5 million. He claims that the double hip replacement you performed added 4 strokes to his golf game."

"Ya gotta hand it to him. Nobody loves this game more than Pete."

To remind himself to keep his head down when
swinging, Jerry relied on a photo of
Jennifer Lopez.

Nobody ever looked up and saw a good shot.

Don Herold

Hugh tries out his new Swiss Army Golf Clubs.

"It's based on the same aerodynamic principle
as the golf ball. The dimple pattern
makes it 27 percent more fuel efficient."

Ted learns an important lesson: Never let your
stomach growl when a member of your foursome
has a 3-foot putt for eagle.

Having narrowly missed a hole-in-one last August,
Phil vowed not to take off his "lucky" shirt
until he did fire an ace.

Dwayne's playing partners quickly tired of his
reliance on his new Miracle Golf video.

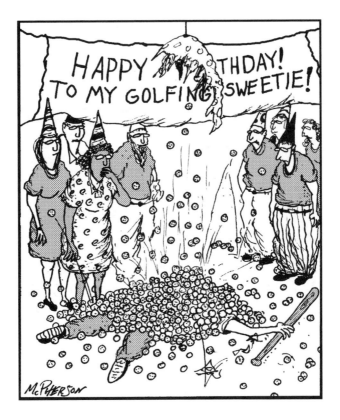

Darren's new 1,200 RPM shoulder-mounted fan
added 30 yards to his drives.

"But Honey, there simply isn't enough room.
I'm sure one of the other rafts can
squeeze you in somehow."

"Will you relax?! They told us to look after the kids while they went to the craft fair. So we're looking after the kids, right?"

"Of all the low-down, dirty, rotten tricks!
I figured I was 210 yards away so I hit
my 5-wood!"

My handicap? Woods and irons.

Chris Codiroli

For those truly agonizing rounds,
Titleist introduces its new edible golf bag.

"Oh, that. I told the kids it was OK for them to use
your golf clubs to play Three Musketeers."

"Yes! It went in! Finally, I got a hole-in-one!
And with THREE witnesses!"

I know I'm getting better at golf because I'm hitting fewer spectators.

Gerald R. Ford

"Don't you see? You slice because you are punishing yourself for having glued your aunt's shoes to the floor when you were twelve."

"NO! Larry! Don't do it! Come back! Larry!
Get back here . . . !"

To psyche out his opponents, Dave's new golf cart came with a "Squealing Wheel" setting.

Barry tries out his new $1,200 slice corrector.

I don't say my golf game is bad but if I grew tomatoes they'd come up sliced.

Anonymous

"His wife told him he was dead meat if he didn't get the new faucet installed today, but there was no way he was going to miss this tournament."

Golf Times magazine unveils its new
Beverage Cart Babes calendar.

"This explains the screams we heard
coming from the foursome in front of us."

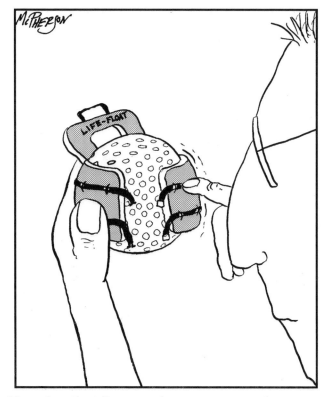

Knowing that it was a long way over the water
hole, Rex took no chances with a $4 golf ball.

If I had cleared the trees and drove the green, it would've been a great shot.

Sam Snead

Nick hoped that the scope on his driver
would put an end to his horrendous slice.

Told by his golf instructor to "be the ball,"
Ron visualizes his upcoming putt.

"The salesman said that these provide three times
the traction of regular golf shoes!"

"No. 2, step forward and take three full swings."

"If he pulls this off we're never
going to hear the end of it."

*But you don't have to go up in the stands and play
your foul balls. I do.*

Sam Snead, to Ted Williams, arguing which was
more difficult, to hit a moving baseball
or a stationary golf ball

CHICKEN SOUP FOR THE SOUL

Business at Zeke's Driving Range tripled since it
added the exploding ceramic statues.

Though it gave him no technological advantage,
Dan loved to intimidate his opponents with
his homemade putter.

"Quit whimpering! You lost the bet fair and square!
And remember, each of our drives has to go at
least 180 yards or it doesn't count."

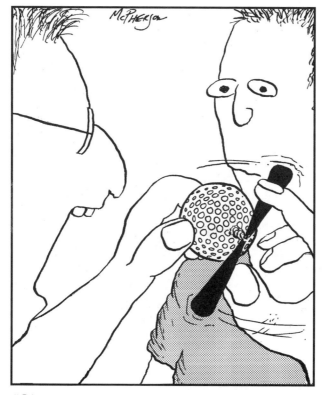

"Oh, yeah? Well you show me where in the
PGA rule book it says I can't
use a ball like this."

Glenn proudly shows off his new Caddy-Cap.™

If Tiger Woods had gone into any other career.

I'm trying as hard as I can, and sometimes things don't go your way, and that's the way things go.

Tiger Woods

Kevin didn't exactly exude confidence when it came to driving over water hazards.

From time to time, just to unnerve his opponents,
Jerry liked to wash his glass eye in a ballwasher.

"Most people find this hole particularly challenging."

*It took me seventeen years to get three thousand hits in baseball.
I did it in one afternoon on the golf course.*

Hank Aaron

Swing hard in case you actually hit the ball.

Dan Marino

"It's been specially trained to gobble up and
then spit out up to ten golf balls per cast."

Jerry's habit of relaxing with his Zen garden
before each putt soon began to perturb
his playing partners.

Kevin finally found a way to keep his
head down when he swings.

Hoping to cure him of his golf addiction, Ted's wife
installs an invisible electric fence system.

Designs for golf's new oversized drivers have
begun to spiral out of control.

Anytime a golfer hits a ball perfectly straight with a big club it is, in my view, a fluke.

Jack Nicklaus

Jerry lands in one of Pinehurst Country Club's
infamous snake traps.

"For heaven's sake! I heard there was
a chance of golf-ball-sized hail, but I
never though I'd live to see the day!"

"Fire one more warning round over their heads,
and if they still don't let us play through,
take out their cart."

"It's U.L. approved, plus it's guaranteed
for up to 50,000 volts!"

As they approached the foursome in front of them, Phil and Bob sensed that they were in for a slow round of golf.

Golf is a game in which the slowest people in the world are in front of you, and the fastest are those behind.

Anonymous

"He's not much at driving, but he's got
a deadly short game."

READER/CUSTOMER CARE SURVEY

CE7S

We care about your opinions! Please take a moment to fill out our online Reader Survey at **http://survey.hcibooks.com**. As a **"THANK YOU"** you will receive a **VALUABLE INSTANT COUPON** towards future book purchases as well as a **SPECIAL GIFT** available only online! Or, you may mail this card back to us and we will send you a copy of our exciting catalog with your valuable coupon inside.

First Name	MI.	Last Name

Address		

State	Zip	Email	City

1. Gender
☐ Female   ☐ Male

2. Age
☐ 8 or younger
☐ 9-12   ☐ 13-16
☐ 17-20   ☐ 21-30
☐ 31+

3. Did you receive this book as a gift?
☐ Yes   ☐ No

4. Annual Household Income
☐ under $25,000
☐ $25,000 - $34,999
☐ $35,000 - $49,999
☐ $50,000 - $74,999
☐ over $75,000

5. What are the ages of the children living in your house?
_____
_____
_____
_____

6. Marital Status
☐ Single
☐ Married
☐ Divorced
☐ Widowed

Comments

Do you have your own Chicken Soup story that you would like to send us?

Arnie has the misfortune of hitting into one of the course's challenging new sickle traps.

Seeing another player's ball land nearby,
Craig quickly put on his "golf ball in the
forehead" bandanna.

"OK, Howard. We'll play two more rounds
using the training clubs, and if all goes well,
you'll play your first solo round on Wednesday."

"It's called 'Spring-A-Swing.' Yesterday he sliced a drive that went in one side of a Winnebago and out the other."

*What goes up must come down. But don't expect it to
come down where you can find it.*

Lily Tomlin

Debbie sends Roger a subtle hint.

"OK, boys! Let's find out once and for all which brand of golf ball really does go the farthest!"

Fortunately, Hal just happened to have a
tree wedge in his bag.

While most people shuddered at the sight of the golf ball-sized hail, Bruce saw it as an opportunity to hone his wedge-shot skills.

Inspired by the success of oversized drivers,
many other golf equipment manufacturers
have followed suit.

The trouble is that most of us find with the modern matched sets of clubs is that they don't really seem to know any more about the game than the old ones did!

Robert Browning, *A History of Golf*

Bert's undercarriage golf club rack allowed him
to sneak off for a round of golf without
arousing his wife's suspicion.

"Help me play a little prank on my husband.
Start walking away with these while exclaiming that you can't
believe you bought a set of new graphite clubs for 10 bucks."

After hitting seven consecutive shots into the
pond, Rick began to show a hint of apathy
toward his golf game.

With an insurmountable lead against his old fraternity
brothers, Jerry twists the knife by letting the beverage
cart girl play out the last three holes for him.

Dennis was able to add 40 yards to his drives
by wheeling around the poster of his boss.

"Ron used to just throw his clubs into a pond.
Now he feels he gets more closure this way."

Equipped with a canister of compressed air and
some rubber tubing, Wayne was able to shave
six strokes off his game.

*I have a tip that can take five strokes off anyone's game.
It's called an eraser.*

Arnold Palmer

Out hiking alone one day, professional golf
announcer Fred Dornquist makes a grave
misstep and is never heard from again.

Dennis shows off his new Clapper™
activated golf bag.

A woman I know is engaged to a real golf nut. They are supposed to get married next Saturday . . . but only if it rains.

Cindy Garner

"I tell ya, Phil, he's actually a pretty decent guy!
I told him you're having the round of your life,
so he says he's going to let you finish the 18th!"

Desperate to find the cause of his horrific slice,
Wade duct-tapes a Camcorder to his driver.

"The rule book says you gotta play it as it lies.
Quit whining and hit the ball."

Carol sends Dave a clear message.

"OK, which one of you turkeys is playing a Titleist 3?"

A golf ball is like a clock. Always hit it at 6 o'clock and make it go toward 12 o'clock. But make sure you're in the same time zone.

Chi Chi Rodriguez

Every so often, at dusk, golfers reported seeing the
ghost of Henry Milford, who in 1921 missed
a two-footer for a double-eagle.

How has retirement affected my golf game?
A lot more people beat me now.

Dwight David Eisenhower

"Penny and Dan would like to share with you this sculpture, which they created as a symbol of their love and devotion."

"OK, just to recap: five points if you hit the Empire State Building. Ten for the U.N. And 50 if you get one inside the Lincoln Tunnel."

"He says he's added 30 yards to his drives."

The woods are full of long drivers.

Harvey Penick

If you break 100, watch your golf. If you break 80, watch your business.

Joey Adams

With the outcome of the match hanging on this putt, Jim secretly dials Wayne's vibrating pager.

"For the hundredth time, I'm sorry I used your
new Titanium driver to unclog the toilet!"

"Hey you guys, check this out. It says here that
this course was designed by Stephen King."

Bruce and Phil quickly regretted betting
$25 a hole with The Great Rinaldo.

"Worst slice I ever saw."

"You're allowed to ask any question about mankind, and THAT'S what you want to know?! OK, you would have finished 1 under par if you hadn't been hit by lightning."

*When it comes to the game of life,
I figure I've played the whole course.*

Lee Trevino

Who Is Jack Canfield?

Jack Canfield is one of America's leading experts in the development of human potential and personal effectiveness. He is both a dynamic, entertaining speaker and a highly sought-after trainer. Jack has a wonderful ability to inform and inspire audiences toward increased levels of self-esteem and peak performance.

He is the author and narrator of several bestselling audio- and video-cassette programs, including *Self-Esteem and Peak Performance, How to Build High Self-Esteem, Self-Esteem in the Classroom* and *Chicken Soup for the Soul—Live.* He is regularly seen on television shows such as *Good Morning America, 20/20* and *NBC Nightly News.* Jack has coauthored numerous books, including the *Chicken Soup for the Soul* series, *Dare to Win* and *The Aladdin Factor* (all with Mark Victor Hansen), *100 Ways to Build Self-Concept in the Classroom* (with Harold C. Wells), *Heart at Work* (with Jacqueline Miller) and *The Power of Focus* (with Les Hewitt and Mark Victor Hansen).

For further information about Jack's books, tapes and training programs, or to schedule him for a presentation, please contact:

Jack Canfield
P.O. Box 30880
Santa Barbara, CA 93130
phone: 805-563-2935 • fax: 805-563-2945
Web site: *www.chickensoup.com*